London: H M S O

HMSO

HMSO publications are available from:

HMSO Publications Centre
(Mail and telephone orders only)
PO Box 276, London, SW8 5DT
Telephone orders 071-873 9090
General enquiries 071-873 0011
(queuing system in operation for both numbers)

HMSO Bookshops
49 High Holborn, London, WC1V 6HB   071-873 0011 (counter service only)
258 Broad Street, Birmingham, B1 2HE   021-643 3740
Southey House, 33 Wine Street, Bristol, BS1 2BQ   (0272) 264306
9-21 Princess Street, Manchester, M60 8AS   061-834 7201
80 Chichester Street, Belfast, BT1 4JY   (0232) 238451
71 Lothian Road, Edinburgh, EH3 9AZ   031-228 4181

HMSO's Accredited Agents
(see Yellow Pages)
and through good booksellers

Photo Credits

Numbers refer to the pages in the illustration section (1–8); Mansell Collection, p. 1; Rex Features, pp. 2 (top), 3 (bottom), 5 (top); John Smith, p. 3 (top); Labour Party, p. 4 (top); Conservative Party, p. 4 (bottom), p. 8 (bottom); Electoral Reform Society, p. 5 (bottom); Press Association, pp. 6 and 7. Page 2 (bottom) is Crown Copyright.

Contents

Introduction

The British system of parliamentary government depends on the electorate voting freely and in secret at periodic elections. Voters choose between rival candidates who usually represent organised political parties with different views. The leader of the party which wins most seats at a general election, or which has the support of a majority in the new House of Commons, is by convention invited by the monarch to form a government. He or she becomes Prime Minister and chooses the ministers who will together form the Government. The Government has to maintain majority support to remain in office and it is responsible, through the House of Commons, to the electorate.

A general election, for all seats in the House of Commons, takes place at least every five years. However, Parliament is usually dissolved—by the Queen acting on the advice of the Prime Minister—and an election called before the end of the full five-year term. The most recent general election was in June 1987. If a seat becomes vacant in the period between general elections (following, for example, the death or resign-ation of a Member of Parliament—an 'MP'), a by-election is held.

The simple majority system of voting is used in parlia-mentary elections throughout Britain.[1] This means that the

---

[1] The term 'Britain' is used informally in this pamphlet to mean the United Kingdom of Great Britain and Northern Ireland. 'Great Britain' comprises England, Scotland and Wales.

candidate with the largest number of votes in each constituency is elected, although he or she may not necessarily have received more votes than all the other candidates combined. The same system is used in local government elections and elections to the European Parliament, except in Northern Ireland, where elections are held under a system of proportional representation.

Britain, like other member countries of the European Community, has been sending directly elected representatives to the European Parliament since 1979. Elections are held every five years; the most recent election was in June 1989.

Extension of the Right to Vote

Although the origins of the British Parliament date from medieval times, elections at which all adult men and women have the franchise (the legal right to vote) are a comparatively recent development.

The first legislation to make the House of Commons more representative was the Reform Act of 1832. This abolished parliamentary seats representing areas with almost no inhabitants and distributed them to more populated areas, taking account of the movement of people from rural areas to the expanding industrial towns. The right to vote was put on a more consistent footing, based on the ownership of property. However, the great majority of the population, including all women, remained without the franchise.

The Representation of the People Act 1867 extended the franchise by adding nearly a million voters to the electorate. However, the right to vote continued to depend on a property qualification, and women were still excluded from the franchise. There was also a further redistribution of seats from less populated to more populated areas. The secret ballot was introduced by the Ballot Act 1872. The Corrupt and Illegal Practices Act 1883 made bribery and other corrupt practices at elections criminal offences.

In 1884 the Franchise Act extended the vote to most male adults. However, the franchise was limited to those with a year's residence qualification. University graduates, and those owning land or business premises in a constituency other than that in which they lived, were allowed a vote in more than one constituency.

The Representation of the People Act 1918 gave the vote to nearly all the categories of men aged 21 and over still excluded from the franchise and lowered the residence qualifications to six months. For the first time women were given the vote, although this was restricted to those aged 30 and over. In 1928 the franchise was extended to all women aged 21 and over.

The Representation of the People Act 1949 abolished additional votes for university graduates and those owning business premises and land in constituencies other than those in which they lived. The six-months residence qualification was removed. In 1969 the minimum voting age was reduced to 18 for men and women. The Representation of the People Acts of 1985 and 1989 gave large numbers of British citizens living abroad the right to vote (see p. 11).

Parliamentary Constituencies

Britain is divided into 650 parliamentary constituencies. Each of these is a geographical area whose inhabitants elect one member to the House of Commons. Constituency boundaries are approved by Parliament following reviews by the Boundary Commissions.[1]

Boundary Commissions

There are four parliamentary Boundary Commissions—for England, Scotland, Wales and Northern Ireland. They are politically impartial. Every 10 to 15 years they conduct reviews of all parliamentary constituencies and European parliamentary constituencies. In the light of these they recommend any redistribution of seats that may seem necessary due to population movements or other changes, including new local government boundaries. They also prepare separate reports on particular constituencies between general reviews. In making recommendations the Commissions must take account of local factors, including local government boundaries, without allowing too great a difference between the size of electorates in constituencies.

---

[1] Britain will comprise 651 constituencies at the next general election, following an interim review by the Boundary Commission for England. An extra constituency is to be created for Milton Keynes, Buckinghamshire (see p. 7).

The Speaker of the House of Commons nominally chairs each of the Commissions, with a senior judge acting as deputy. Two other members are appointed by government ministers, usually after the other political parties have been consulted. With the exception of the Speaker, no MP may be a member of the Boundary Commissions.

A number of people are appointed by law to advise the Commissions. These are: The Registrar-General for England and Wales; The Registrar-General of Births, Deaths and Marriages in Scotland; and the Director-General of the Ordnance Survey. In Northern Ireland they are the Chief Electoral Officer, the Registrar-General of Births, Deaths and Marriages, and the Commissioner of Valuation.

Review Procedure

Following the Commission's publication of any recommendations in a constituency, a month is allowed for different views to be put forward.[2] A local inquiry has to be held if one of the local authorities affected, or 100 or more electors in the constituency concerned, make representations. If the recommendations are changed they must be published but, if they are opposed again, a further local inquiry does not have to be held. The final recommendations are submitted to the relevant Secretary of State, who must then put the report before Parliament, together with a draft Order in Council giving effect to the recommendations. The recommendations may be altered by the Secretary of State but, if so, he or she must give reasons.

---

[2] The Government has announced that it intends to increase this period to two months.

Numbers of Constituencies

The last general reports of the Commissions for England, Wales and Scotland were approved by Parliament in 1983. The last report for Northern Ireland was approved in 1982. As a result of the Commissions' recommendations, the number of parliamentary constituencies in Britain was increased from 635 to 650. The increases were as follows: in England, from 516 to 523; in Scotland, from 71 to 72; in Wales, from 36 to 38; and in Northern Ireland, from 12 to 17.

In addition to continuing movements in population, these changes reflected the major organisation of local government areas in the 1970s and the growth in the size of the electorate, largely due to the lowering of the voting age in 1969 (see p. 4).

Electoral Quotas

The number of electors in a constituency must be as near as possible to the electoral quota. This figure is obtained by dividing the total electorate of England, Scotland, Wales or Northern Ireland by the number of constituencies in that part of Britain at the beginning of the review.

In 1990 the electoral quotas were: England 69,577; Scotland 54,676; Wales 58,093; and Northern Ireland 66,506. The parliamentary constituency with the largest electorate in Britain is Milton Keynes, with 109,839 (see footnote to p. 5), and the constituency with the smallest is the Western Isles in Scotland, with 23,084. The total electorate in Britain on the 1990 register is nearly 43·7 million.

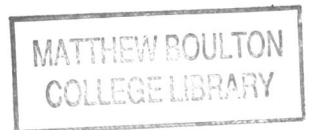

Changes in Electoral Law

Questions concerning changes in electoral law are considered periodically at a Speaker's Conference, which consists of MPs meeting under the chairmanship of the Speaker. As with other parliamentary committees, the party composition of the Conference reflects that of the House. The proceedings are in private and recommendations are published in the form of letters from the Speaker to the Prime Minister. Five such conferences have been held this century, the last in 1978.

Voters and Candidates

Who May Vote

British citizens are entitled to vote at parliamentary elections provided that they are aged 18 or over and are not subject to any legal incapacity to vote. Citizens of other Commonwealth countries and the Irish Republic may also vote at parliamentary elections if they are resident in Britain, aged 18 or over and are not subject to any legal incapacity to vote. To be entitled to vote in a constituency, electors have to be registered in the electoral register of the constituency as resident on a qualifying date, unless they are resident abroad (see p. 11). These dates are 10 October in England, Scotland and Wales and 15 September in Northern Ireland. In Northern Ireland a person must also have been continuously resident in the constituency for three months ending on the qualifying date. The new register comes into force on 16 February each year and includes young people who will reach voting age during the year; the date of their eighteenth birthday is listed.

Registration of Voters

The electoral register for each constituency is prepared annually by electoral registration officers. In England and Wales these are chief executives, or other senior officers, of local government authorities. The electoral registration officer in Scotland is normally the regional valuation assessor. In Northern Ireland the register is compiled by the Chief Electoral Officer.

In order to find out the names of the people in an area who are qualified to be registered, the registration officer sends a form to every household each year. The householder is required to give details of all occupants who are eligible to vote. Alternatively, representatives of the registration officer may call at all households. Individuals who do not give the required information, or who give false information, may be fined. Provisional electors lists or draft registers of voters are displayed in council offices, main post offices and public libraries, from 28 November to 16 December. Objections can be raised; the final decision is made by the registration officer, subject to appeal to the county court or, in Scotland, the sheriff court. A similar procedure is followed in Northern Ireland.

Copies of the final register are normally available in public libraries and some other public offices in each constituency.

Voting in elections is voluntary; at the last general election in 1987 just over 75 per cent of the electorate voted.

Who May Not Vote

The following people are not entitled to vote in parliamentary elections:

—peers, and peeresses in their own right, who are members of the House of Lords;[1]

—young people under 18 years of age;

—foreign nationals other than citizens of the Irish Republic resident in Britain (citizens of Commonwealth countries may vote—see p. 9);

[1] Members of the House of Lords may vote in local government elections.

—patients detained under mental health legislation;

—sentenced prisoners; and

—people convicted within the previous five years of corrupt or illegal election practices.

British Electors Overseas

A further group of some 2 million British citizens living abroad are now eligible to register as electors. Under the Representation of the People Act 1985 the right to vote was extended to British citizens resident abroad, for a period of five years after they have left Britain. The Representation of the People Act 1989 has extended the period during which people may register to vote to 20 years after leaving Britain. It also enfranchised people who were too young to register as electors before they left Britain. Overseas electors may register and vote only in the constituency in which they were last resident. They may vote by proxy at elections to the British and European Parliaments. At present nearly 35,000 British citizens resident abroad are registered to vote in parliamentary elections. Members of the armed forces, Crown servants such as embassy officials, and staff of the British Council who are employed overseas, and their husbands and wives, also have the right to vote in elections in Britain, regardless of how long they have been abroad.

How Electors Vote

In general, electors have to vote at the polling station allotted to them by the returning officer. However, special arrangements exist for electors who are likely to be away during the period of an election. They may apply for a postal or a proxy vote;

the latter is a vote which is cast by a person authorised to vote on another's behalf. Postal ballot papers can be sent only to addresses in Britain.

People who cannot reasonably be expected to vote in person at the polling station, for whatever reason, may apply for an absent vote at particular elections. Those who are unable to attend polling stations due to physical incapacity, nature of work and, in some cases, distance from the polling station, may apply to be put on a permanent list of absent voters. In addition, electors who change address during the period for which the electoral register is valid may apply to be treated as absent voters until the next register comes into force.

Candidates

Any man or woman who is a British citizen, or a citizen of another Commonwealth country or the Irish Republic, may stand as a candidate at a parliamentary election provided he or she is aged 21 or over and is not disqualified in any way. Those disqualified from election include the following:

—undischarged bankrupts;

—people sentenced to more than one year's imprisonment;

—clergy of the Church of England, Church of Scotland, Church of Ireland and Roman Catholic Church;

  members of the House of Lords; and

—people holding offices listed in the House of Commons Disqualification Act 1975. This includes judges, civil servants, some local government officers, members of the regular armed forces or the police service, some members of public corporations and government commissions, and members of the parliaments or assemblies of countries outside the Commonwealth.

Candidates normally belong to one of the main political parties, although smaller parties and groups also put forward candidates, and individuals may stand without party support. Candidates do not have to be resident in the constituencies for which they stand.

Most candidates are selected by the party organisation in the constituency through its selection committee, which interviews applicants before choosing a candidate. The national organisations of the Conservative and Labour parties keep lists of approved candidates, but the constituency parties are free to choose people who are not on the lists. Once selected, candidates have to be approved by the national party organisation before being adopted as the 'prospective' candidate for the constituency. Candidates usually make themselves known to voters in the constituency and involve themselves in local affairs before the opening of the election campaign.

Candidates who are on the electoral register may vote in their constituencies.

In the 1987 general election a total of 2,325 candidates stood for the 650 constituencies. Of these, 82 per cent belonged to the three main national parties, each of which put up 633 candidates, contesting all seats other than the 17 in Northern Ireland. (The Conservative total includes the Speaker of the House of Commons who, before his election as Speaker, was a Conservative MP.)

Calling an Election

Electoral procedures in Britain are based principally on the Representation of the People Acts 1983 and 1985.

When a decision has been taken to dissolve Parliament, the following orders are made by the Queen in Council:

—The Lord Chancellor is directed to affix the Great Seal to the royal proclamation for dissolving the old and calling the new Parliament; and

—The Lord Chancellor and Secretary of State for Northern Ireland are directed to issue the Writs of Election.

The writs are normally issued on the same day as the proclamation summoning the new Parliament.

It is usual for the Prime Minister to announce the dissolution of Parliament and to explain the reasons for holding the election. Polling takes place within 17 days of the dissolution, not including week-ends, bank holidays and days of public thanksgiving or mourning.

If the monarch dies after the dissolution of Parliament, polling day is postponed for two weeks.

By-elections

By-elections take place when a parliamentary seat falls vacant between general elections (see pp. 1 and 53). When a by-election is to be held, the Speaker of the House of Commons issues a warrant to the Clerk of the Crown directing the Clerk to issue a Writ of Election. The writ is usually issued on the same day as the Speaker's warrant. If a vacancy occurs while Parliament is meeting, the motion for a new writ is usually moved by the party to which the former MP belonged. If the House is not meeting, the Speaker can issue a warrant if two MPs certify that a seat is vacant and notice is given in *The London Gazette.*

By-elections in individual constituencies are regarded as tests of national opinion in the period between general elections. By-election campaigns receive extensive coverage in the press and on radio and television. The results are much discussed by senior politicians and political commentators, who use the voting figures to speculate on the likely result of the next general election and the popularity of the parties' policies.

Administration of Elections

The Home Office (in England and Wales), the Scottish Home and Health Department and the Northern Ireland Office are responsible for overseeing electoral law. Elections in England and Wales are administered by the returning officer (the sheriff of the county, the mayor of a London borough or the chairman of a district council). In practice, the duties are carried out by an acting returning officer. In Scotland, returning officers are normally the chief executives or directors of administration of the regional or islands council.[1] In Northern Ireland, the Chief Electoral Officer is the returning officer for all constituencies.

---

[1] On the mainland of Scotland local government is on a two-tier basis: nine regional councils, which are divided into 53 district councils. Orkney, Shetland and the Western Isles, because of their separation from the Scottish mainland, have single, all-purpose authorities known as islands councils.

The individual elections for each constituency are run by full-time deputies who also perform other functions.

Returning officers publish, normally by means of posters in public places, notices of election, which give the date of the election and the names of the candidates. They also send an official poll card to all electors on the register, which sets out the following:

—the name of the constituency;

—the elector's name, address, and number on the register;

—the address of the elector's polling station; and

—the date and hours of the poll.

Returning officers also:

—arrange the printing of the ballot papers;

—see that there are enough polling stations;

—provide ballot boxes and other equipment for the polling stations and ensure that each is provided with compartments to safeguard the secrecy of the vote;

—appoint and pay the staff at the polling stations (a presiding officer and a certain number of poll clerks); and

—organise the counting of votes.

Most of the staff involved in the above work are local government employees, temporarily transferred from other work. In addition, others are employed for the day. School teachers often act as polling clerks since many schools have a

holiday on election day while the buildings are used as polling stations. Bank clerks often assist in counting the votes.

The official expenses of a parliamentary election, as distinct from candidates' expenses (see pp. 32–4), are paid by the Government.

Nomination of Candidates

Candidates must be nominated on official nomination papers, giving their full name and home address. A political or personal description of up to six words may be included. The nomination paper must be signed by ten electors including a proposer and a seconder. Candidates must consent in writing to their nomination.

At general elections, nomination papers must be delivered during the period between the publication of the notice of election and six days after the proclamation summoning the new Parliament, between the hours of 10.00 and 16.00 each day. The procedure is the same at by-elections, except that the last day is fixed by the returning officer and must be between the third day after the publication of the notice and the seventh day after the writ is received. By the end of the period for delivering the nomination papers the name and address of the election agent for each candidate must be declared to the returning officer. If the agent is anyone other than the candidate, the declaration must be made by the agent or accompanied by a written note of acceptance.

A sum of £500 must be deposited on behalf of each candidate during the period allowed for delivery of nomination papers. If candidates receive at least 5 per cent of the total votes cast, their deposit is returned; if not, their deposit is lost.

The deposit is intended to ensure that candidates are seriously seeking election. At the 1987 election only one candidate from the three main national parties failed to get 5 per cent of the vote and thereby lost the deposit.

Candidates may withdraw from the election up to the end of the time for the delivery of nomination papers. Notice of withdrawal must be signed by the candidate and a witness and delivered to the returning officer.

People may make objections about nominations to the returning officer during the last day for the delivery of nominations, until an hour after nominations close. The returning officer decides whether objections are valid. Among those who may object to the validity of a nomination paper are candidates, their election agents, their proposers and their seconders.

Once any objections have been dealt with, the returning officer publishes the names of the candidates nominated, together with those of the proposers and seconders.

Polling Day

At general elections polling day is the eleventh working day after the last day for delivery of nomination papers. At by-elections polling is between the ninth and eleventh day after the end of the period for the delivery of the nomination papers.

If a candidate dies between the publication of nominations and the poll, or after the poll has begun and before the result is declared, the procedure begins again. The election is held as though the writ had been received 28 days after the returning officer received proof of death.

General elections are usually held on Thursdays, although the Prime Minister is free to choose a different day.

Timetable for General Elections

The five formal stages of general elections are:

1. royal proclamation;

2. issue of writs, as soon as possible after the royal proclamation—usually the same day;

3. publication of the notice of election, not later than the second day after the writ is received;

4. delivery of nomination papers, not later than the sixth day after the royal proclamation; and

5. polling day, on the eleventh day after the last day for delivery of nomination papers (that is, about three to four weeks after the election is announced).

The Election Campaign

General election campaigns take place at both national and constituency levels. The main parties hold national press conferences each day during the campaign, chaired by the leader or other leading members of the party. These are widely reported in the media, as are other aspects of the campaign. Party leaders also tour the country, while candidates and local party workers campaign in individual constituencies.

Election Agents and Local Parties

Each parliamentary candidate appoints an election agent, who is responsible for running the campaign and, in particular, for controlling expenses.[1] Agents should be familiar with electoral law and practice. They may be paid for their services but, if so, this must be included in the maximum amount allowed for a candidate's expenses. They may also employ paid polling agents, clerks and messengers, within the limits of the election expenses, although in practice most local parties rely on volunteers and choose to concentrate their limited campaign expenditure on publicity.

Some agents are full-time salaried officials who act as party organisers in one or more constituencies in the period between elections. They are normally paid by local constituency parties,

---

[1] Candidates may act as their own agents but normally do not do so, except in the case of independent and minor party candidates.

although the Labour Party head office contributes to the cost of 28 agents in key constituencies. Many more agents work on a part-time or voluntary basis. Individual parties organise training courses in electoral law and related matters for agents.

Members of each constituency or local party support the campaigns of parliamentary candidates. This involves raising funds, clerical work, preparing and distributing publicity materials and canvassing electors. Any number of unpaid workers may help with the campaign.

Committee Rooms

At the beginning of the election campaign agents arrange for committee rooms to be made available for the use of the party organisation in the constituency: in some cases the major parties maintain permanent offices. The rooms are used as headquarters for speakers, canvassers, messengers and others involved in the election campaign. They are also used for sending out election addresses and leaflets and as a base for briefing the candidate on the latest news about political developments.

Publications and Advertising

All the main political parties produce a wide range of publicity material. The publication of such material increases dramatically during election campaigns, although publicity directed at the election of individual candidates is subject to expenditure limits (see pp. 32–4).

The national headquarters of political parties are responsible for preparing party election broadcasts for television and radio (see pp. 25–6). They are also responsible for arranging advertising for the party as a whole. Paying for political advertising on radio and television is not permitted, but political advertising is allowed in the press: during the 1987 election campaign a total of 336 pages of political advertising appeared in the national newspapers. The parties also arrange for posters to appear in prominent places, such as busy road junctions. The major parties receive advice on these matters from leading advertising agencies or advertising professionals.

Local Publicity
In individual constituencies local parties are responsible for preparing leaflets and posters. The main form of publicity at constituency level is each candidate's election address, which can be sent free to every household in the constituency. This typically includes a photograph of the candidate, some biographical details, and a message to the electors setting out reasons for voting for the candidate and the party he or she represents. A survey of voters in the 1987 general election found that 94 per cent remembered receiving election publicity material and 49 per cent read an election address, suggesting that such publicity was the electorate's main point of contact with the local party organisations.

Part of the election address often takes the form of a small poster urging people to vote for the candidate. The posters are usually in the party colours—blue for the Conservative Party, red for the Labour Party and orange or gold for the Liberal Democrats. They usually bear the candidate's name and may show the party's symbols. Individual voters often display the posters in the windows of their homes. Local parties also arrange the distribution of larger posters for display.

In addition to election addresses local parties produce a variety of publications during elections, subject to the limits on expenditure. It is usually too expensive to distribute more than just the election address to all constituents during general elections, but further material can be delivered, by party workers or by post, to selected voters. An increasing number of local parties have access to computers which make it easier to 'target' voters identified by canvassers as potential supporters. Particular categories of voters can also be selected in this way.

All orders for printing and advertising in constituency campaigns must be given by candidates or their agents. Unauthorised people are guilty of corrupt practice if they pay for publicity materials to promote the election of a candidate. The name and address of the printer and publisher must be on all bills, leaflets and similar material. No one may be paid to display them, except for advertising agents in the ordinary course of business.

The Media

Election campaigns are extensively covered by all the media in Britain. Campaign coverage dominates the national newspapers, while television and radio offer special election programmes as well as extending their existing news programmes to cover the election.

The Press

Britain's newspapers and magazines are all privately owned and represent a range of political viewpoints, decided by owners and editors; the newspapers are almost always financially independent of the political parties. By the end of the 1987 general election campaign seven of the eleven major national daily newspapers had come out in support of the Conservative Party, two in favour of the Labour Party and one in favour of a coalition; one newspaper expressed no view. Britain's Sunday newspapers, the regional press and political magazines offered a similar range of views.

Most newspapers cover all aspects of election campaigns. Many publish articles by columnists with views that differ from the newspaper's editorial position. Many also attack certain aspects of the policies of the party they support or acknowledge some good points about parties they do not generally back.

Television and Radio

Television and radio coverage of political matters, including elections, is required to be impartial. Extended news programmes cover all aspects of the major parties' campaigns at national level and in the constituencies. Political parties arrange 'photo opportunities' during which well-known politicians are photographed in such places as factories, farms, building sites and youth centres. They often use such visits to make points about party policies. The resulting news stories feature prominently on television, as do excerpts from speeches by key politicians.

Special election programmes include discussions between politicians belonging to the rival parties; often a studio audience of members of the public is able to challenge and question senior politicians. Radio 'phone-ins' also allow ordinary callers to question, or put their views to, political leaders. Broadcast coverage also includes interviews with leading figures from all the parties, reports focusing on particular election issues, and commentaries from political journalists.

The use of transmitting stations outside Britain for election propaganda is prohibited unless the arrangements are made with the public bodies responsible for broadcasting (or a programme contractor).

Candidates may take part in an election campaign programme about their constituency only if all their rival candidates take part or agree that the programme may go ahead.

Party Political Broadcasting

Arrangements for party election broadcasts on radio and television during general elections are made by a committee consisting of representatives of the political parties, the British Broadcasting Corporation (BBC), the Independent Television Commission (ITC) and the Radio Authority.[2] Party election broadcasts are transmitted on BBC and independent television channels. The amount of time each party is allowed depends in part on the number of candidates it has in the election and its strength in the previous Parliament.

The allocation of party election broadcasts for the 1987 general election gave the Conservative and Labour parties and the Liberal-Social Democratic Alliance[3] five national television

[2] The BBC, the ITC and the Radio Authority are the public bodies responsible for television and radio services in Britain. On 1 January 1991 the latter two bodies replaced the former Independent Broadcasting Authority.

[3] The Social Democratic Party was formed in 1981 and made an alliance with the Liberal Party in the same year. The two parties merged in 1988, becoming the Liberal Democrats, formally known as the Social and Liberal Democrats.

broadcasts each. The Green Party made one national television broadcast. The Scottish National Party, Plaid Cymru and the Northern Ireland parties were allocated broadcasts on Scottish, Welsh and Northern Ireland television respectively. In addition to television broadcasts, all the major parties were allocated radio time. In all such broadcasts editorial control rests with the parties.

Canvassing

Canvassing involves local party workers visiting the homes of voters and asking them whether they intend to vote for their party's candidate. During the campaign canvassing can provide candidates and their helpers with valuable information on people's voting intentions and their attitude to particular issues, enabling them to adapt their campaign tactics. During polling day party workers can revisit the homes of those people who have promised to support their parties and, if they have so far failed to vote, urge them to do so.

In practice few constituency parties conduct comprehensive canvasses, as these would involve visits to many thousands of homes in each constituency. The most thorough canvassing tends to take place in marginal constituencies (see pp. 30–31) although the results can often be unreliable, as those interviewed may offer the same assurances of support to canvassers from different parties.

A survey in 1987 found that 16 per cent of voters remembered being approached by one or more of the parties on election day.

Public Meetings

Candidates may hold as many public meetings as they choose. Meetings may be held indoors or outside, provided they are conducted in an orderly manner and do not cause obstruction. In England, Scotland and Wales candidates may use state schools and public halls at reasonable times during the election campaign, although they may have to pay for heating and lighting the rooms, or meet the cost of any damage. In Northern Ireland candidates may not use buildings maintained out of public funds.

Candidates frequently invite guests to speak or attend meetings in their support. Such speakers are often leading members of their parties or well-known personalities, such as actors, writers and entertainers, who are party supporters. The parties' best-known politicians, including government ministers and their opposition counterparts, tend to concentrate their efforts on those marginal constituencies which have been targeted by their parties.

Only a relatively small proportion of the electorate normally attends any of the meetings arranged by the parties during election campaigns. Attendance is often greater at joint meetings of rival candidates arranged by local churches or associations, or at meetings where the speakers include prominent politicians.

Party leaders and other key politicians also speak at large meetings which are not necessarily related to the campaigning in a particular constituency. These events are usually well covered by the media.

Manifestos

All Britain's main political parties publish manifestos during general election campaigns. Usually the result of a considerable amount of work by senior party figures in the period before elections are announced, manifestos are publications which are intended to tell the electorate what the party would do if it formed the next government; they therefore cover party policy on a range of matters. If elected, parties can claim a popular mandate from the voters for policies contained in their manifestos.

Manifestos are usually launched by each of the parties at press conferences in the first week or so of the campaign. They normally have titles which are in the form of slogans, designed to sum up the parties' messages. Thus in 1987 the governing Conservative Party sought re-election under the title *The Next Moves Forward*, in contrast to the Alliance's *Britain United* and the Labour Party's *Britain Will Win*.

Manifestos normally open with forewords by the respective party leaders. They cover party policies in varying degrees of detail but may also set out the parties' past achievements and attack the policies of their opponents. In 1987 the Conservative manifesto had 77 pages, and the Labour manifesto 17.

Although in practice relatively few people read copies of the parties' manifestos, those of the major parties receive extensive publicity in the newspapers and on television and radio. Their themes are also taken up in individual candidates' election addresses. Manifestos thus provide the basis for much of the general election campaign debate.

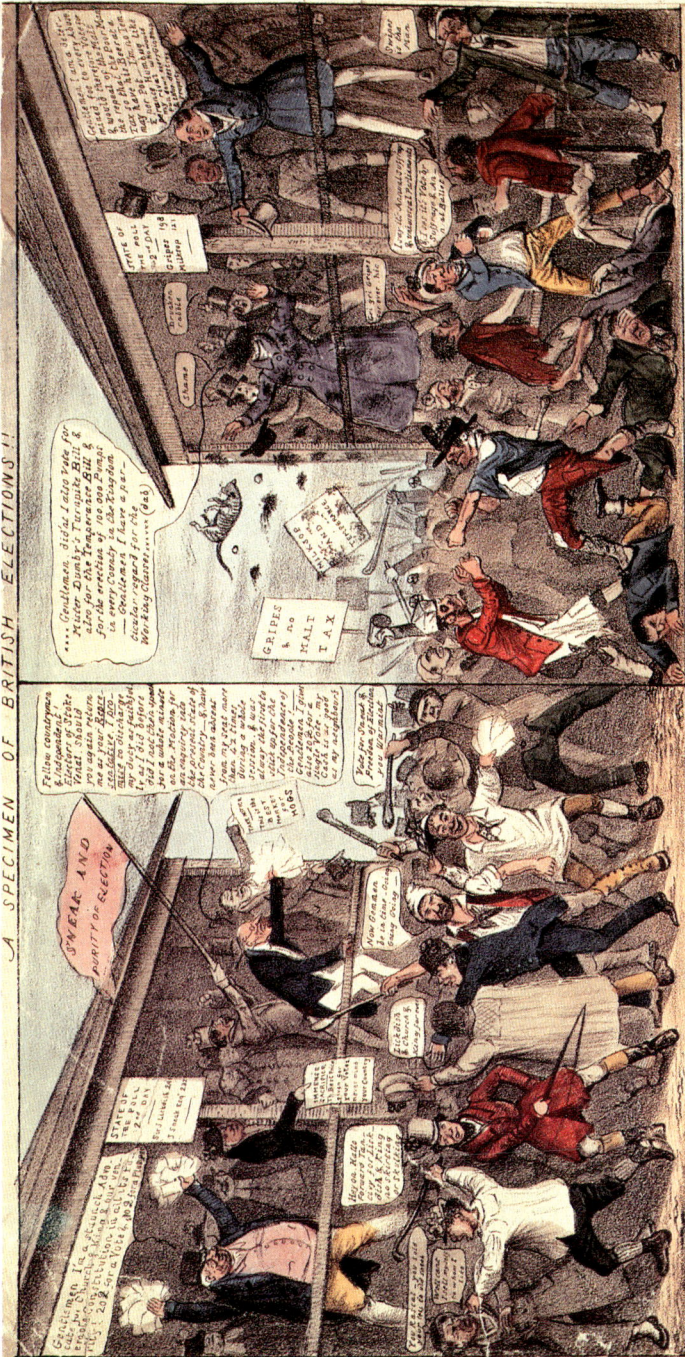

A nineteenth-century cartoon satirising the electoral practices of the time.
Such abuses continued until stricter legislative controls were introduced (see p. 3).

A Conservative Party campaign bus—a typical part of the election scene as the parties compete to gain publicity for their policies and to win the political argument.

Meeting the media—the Labour Party leader, the Right Honourable Neil Kinnock, MP, being interviewed by Independent Television News (ITN).

A Labour candidate and supporters campaigning on the street during a parliamentary by-election.

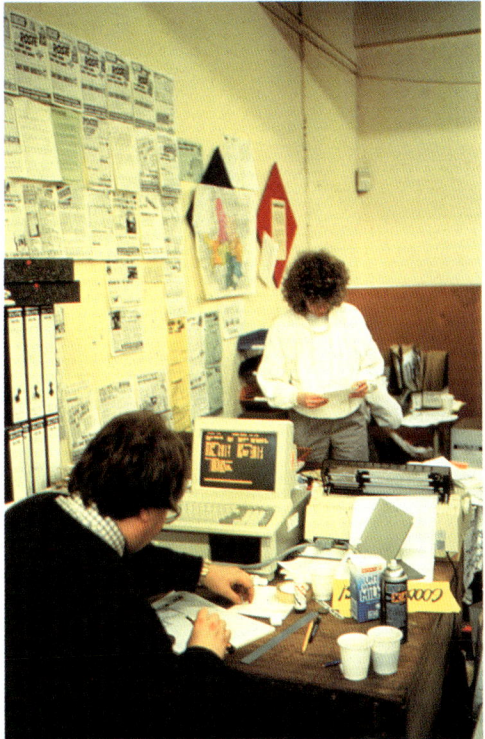

A Liberal-Social Democratic Alliance campaign office in action in the 1987 General Election campaign.

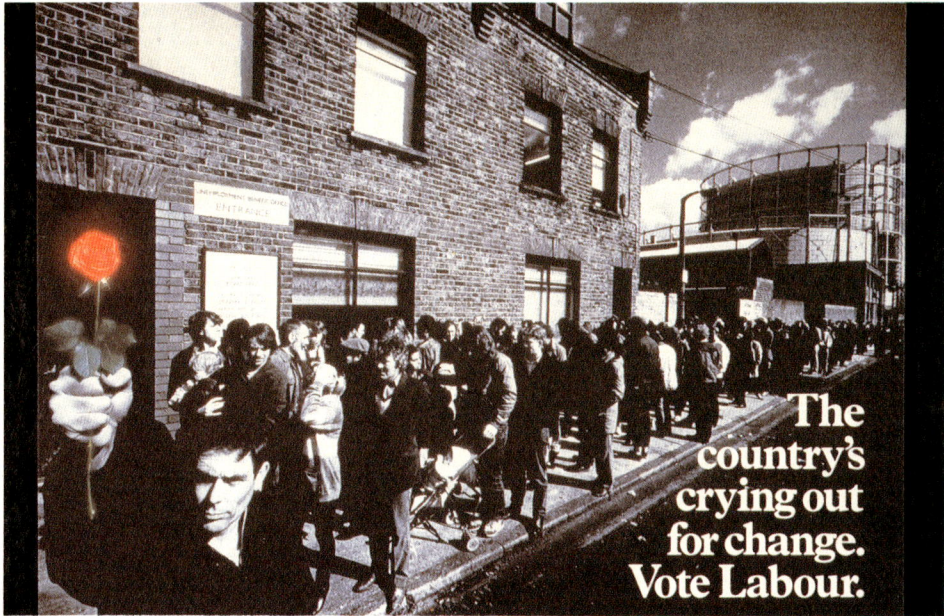

A Labour Party poster.

All the main political parties use a wide range of publicity material, including posters in public places, leaflets and newsletters. These are used to put across their arguments, both during election campaigns and between elections.

An example of Conservative Party publicity material.

● Labour's massive spending plans would mean that much more would have to be taken from ordinary working taxpayers. Independent analysts have estimated that Labour's programme could cost as much as an extra £50 billion every year - enough to double the **basic rate** of income tax.

● Labour have admitted that they would scrap the upper earnings limit on **National Insurance Contributions** - adding an extra 9 per cent to marginal rates of tax and NICs for all those earning more than £18,200 a year.

● The **top rate of tax** would jump to 50 per cent - or 59 per cent when the extra National Insurance is taken into account.

● Labour would introduce three new taxes. **A savings tax** would be introduced on all investment income over £3,000 per year (£5,000 for pensioners). Households would face a **new property tax**, like the old rates, but with much steeper bills. Firms undertaking training programmes deemed by Labour to be inadequate would have to pay a **jobs tax** set at 0.5 per cent of pay roll costs.

The former Prime Minister, the Right Honourable Margaret Thatcher, MP, and her husband entering a polling station to vote during the 1987 General Election.

1	**BROOKE** (Peter Leonard Brooke, of Conservative)	
2	**JONES** (Stephen Phillip Jones, of 37D Ilminster Gardens, London SW11 1PJ, The Labour Party Candidate)	
3	**LITVIN** (Victor Litvin, of 81 Marley Walk, Station Parade, NW2 4PY, Conservative Pro-Nuclear War Gay Rights)	
4	**REEVE** (Anthony Reeve, of 207 Coed-y-Gores, Llanedeyrn, Cardiff CF3 7NL, National Front)	
5	**SHORTER** (Roger Everingham Shorter, of 45 Stalbridge Buildings, Lumley Street, London W1, Ecology Party)	
6	**SPENCE** (Alan Walter Spence, of 35 Russell Chambers, Bury Place, London WC1, Communist Party of Great Britain)	
7	**WALKER-SMITH** (Adrian Anthony Walker-Smith, of 11 Lesley Court, Strutton Ground, London SW1P 2HZ, Liberal/SDP Alliance)	

An example of a ballot paper. Each elector who votes on polling day records his or her vote on the ballot paper (see p. 36).

Votes being counted after polling in a parliamentary by-election. Representatives of the political parties which contested the election may attend the count (see p. 39). Some, wearing rosettes, may be seen on the right of the picture.

The result of a by-election being declared by the returning officer. Rival candidates and their supporters are standing alongside.

Senior Labour Party figures campaigning in the European parliamentary elections in 1984.

Conservatives campaigning during the 1989 elections to the European Parliament.

Election Issues

Election issues are the areas of difference between rival parties on which general elections are contested. The parties' approaches to policy matters are affected by their differing political philosophies and traditions. However, although each of the main parties seeks to offer a full range of policies relating to all aspects of government, in practice only a few areas of policy normally emerge as key issues during election campaigns. These issues normally include policies on the economy and taxation—often regarded as the most important set of issues— health care, education and defence. The personalities and abilities of party leaders can also become issues. Policies towards some matters, such as aspects of foreign policy and the problems of Northern Ireland, are traditionally subject to broad agreement between the main parties and are thus less important as issues.

Pressure Groups

Countless pressure groups are active in Britain, at both national and local level; some also operate internationally. Most seek to influence government policy on a particular issue or a range of related issues. The pressure group Friends of the Earth, for example, has sought to influence policies on the environment. Other organisations are known as interest groups. They seek to advance the interests of particular groups of people or organis- ations. Examples include the Confederation of British Industry (CBI), whose members include many British commercial com- panies; and the trade unions, many of which are linked together in the Trades Union Congress (TUC).

Some pressure groups tend to favour particular political parties and they or their members may offer help during the campaign. However, during election campaigns they may also seek promises of support from candidates on particular issues. The fact that so many candidates are actively seeking support on a range of issues gives pressure groups a good opportunity to air their views.

Safe and Marginal Constituencies

Most of Britain's 650 constituencies are what are often called 'safe seats'. This means that one or other of the main parties has traditionally enjoyed overwhelming support in elections for the seat concerned. As a result an MP seeking re-election for a safe seat or a candidate from the same party seeking election there could normally expect to be returned for that constituency in future elections. Such safe seats are lost only if there is a major decline in the popularity of the party concerned, as sometimes occurs at by-elections (see pp. 14–15).

At present many rural constituencies are safe Conservative seats and, while both the major parties are well represented in towns and cities, most 'safe' Labour seats are in urban areas. There are also regional differences. At the 1987 general election (see p. 51) support for the Conservative Party was greatest in the south of England (with the exception of central London), while that for the Labour Party was greatest in the north of England, Scotland and Wales. Support for the Alliance was fairly evenly distributed.

In practice the outcome of a general election is decided by the results in marginal constituencies. These are seats where, at the previous election, no single party had a large majority.

Thus, if there is a slight fall in the relative popularity of the party holding the seat, a candidate from a rival party would be elected. Following the general election of 1987, for example, there were 151 seats where the winning candidate had a majority of 10 per cent or less of the vote.

All the main parties target particular marginal constituencies and focus their campaigns on winning such seats. Such constituencies are more likely to receive visits by senior politicians and well-known personalities. The candidates and local campaign manager are often in regular contact with party headquarters and the parties may send in extra volunteers and resources from outside the constituency to help during the campaign.

Tactical Voting

Voters usually vote for the candidate and party which they would most like to see win the election. However, they may decide that the party they support has little chance of winning the election in their constituency. Rather than see the party they would least like to win succeed, they may instead choose to vote for a party which has a better chance of winning than their own first choice. Thus a Labour supporter whose candidate normally came third in elections in a safe Conservative seat might decide to vote for a Liberal Democrat candidate who appeared to have a better chance of winning, in the hope of preventing the Conservative candidate from being elected.

This practice is known as tactical voting. It is, however, hard to judge how important—if at all—tactical voting is in general elections.

Opinion Polls

As surveys of the views of the public, opinion polls play a major part in the general election campaign process. Their findings are much discussed by the media and influence the parties' campaigns. During the 1987 general election campaign 73 nationwide surveys were reported in the media, with almost all the national newspapers commissioning their own polls. The media also reported opinion polls which related to particular regions, groups of marginal constituencies and individual seats. In addition the major parties paid for their own private polling.

National opinion polls usually involve samples of 1,000–2,000 people from across the country, selected to represent, as nearly as possible, a cross-section of the electorate. They are normally conducted by independent commercial organisations. People are usually questioned over a period of one to two days. As well as questions on voting intentions, people are often asked about their opinions on a range of political issues and on their attitudes to the different parties' policies. They are also often asked for their views on the standing of the party leaders, and about who would make the best Prime Minister.

Election Expenses

Candidates' election expenses are strictly regulated; breaches of the law are punishable by severe penalties.[4] If the winning candidate is involved, a fresh election may be called.

The maximum sums of money which may be spent by a candidate are:

[4] In December 1989 the Government announced a review of the statutory controls of election expenses.

—in *borough constituencies,*[5] £4,144 plus 3·5 pence for each elector; and

—in *county constituencies,*[6] £4,144 plus 4·7 pence for each elector.

Thus, in an average-sized borough constituency in England the maximum amount which could be spent by a candidate would be almost £6,600, and in an average-sized county constituency in England the maximum would be just over £7,400.

Under the Representation of the People Act 1989 separate, higher limits have been set for spending in by-elections. These reflect the fact that by-elections in individual constituencies are, in practice, often regarded as tests of national opinion in the period between elections (see p. 14). The maximum amounts of money which may be spent are:

—in *borough constituencies,* £16,577 plus 14·1 pence for each elector; and

—in *county constituencies,* £16,577 plus 18·6 pence for each elector.

Candidates may post one communication relating to the election to each household in a constituency free of charge, providing it weighs no more than 57 grammes (2 ounces). This is usually their election address (see p. 22). All other expenses,

[5] Constituencies in densely populated urban areas (burgh constituencies in Scotland).

[6] Constituencies in less densely populated rural areas.

apart from the candidate's personal expenses, are subject to the statutory limit, although a candidate's personal expenses beyond £600 must be paid by the election agent and accounted for in the return of election expenses. No one other than the candidate, election agent or a person authorised in writing by the agent may spend money to secure the election of a candidate. After the election, the agent must make a return of all election expenses to the returning officer within 35 days.

The limits of candidates' expenditure do not apply to the amounts that may be spent by national party organisations on campaigning. They may spend what they like on party political broadcasts, transport for party leaders and general publicity.

Corrupt and Illegal Practices
Certain offences connected with elections committed by candidates or their agents, or with their knowledge and consent, make a candidate's election invalid (or void). These offences are divided into:

—*corrupt practices*, including bribery, treating (giving food, drink, entertainment or provisions in order to influence electors), undue influence, personation (voting in the name of another person), and false declarations concerning election expenses: and

—*other illegal practices*, including illegal payments, illegal employment, illegal hiring of transport or premises, improper conduct of the election campaign, various voting offences, and breaches of the law governing election expenses.

Anyone found guilty by a court of corrupt or illegal practices at elections may be fined or imprisoned and may lose their right to vote or stand for election for up to ten years.

Measures to Prevent Electoral Malpractice
(Northern Ireland only)

Legislation relating exclusively to Northern Ireland and designed to strengthen the safeguards against electoral abuse was passed in 1985. The Elections (Northern Ireland) Act was introduced because of the problem of personation (see p. 34) which had increased dramatically and threatened to undermine the electoral system.

Under the 1985 Act voters have to show a personal document, such as a driving licence or passport, before they are given a ballot paper. Possessing forged documents or documents bearing another person's name for the purpose of personation was made an offence.

The Poll

Each constituency is divided into a number of polling districts (wards in Northern Ireland). In each district or ward there is a polling station. Most are in schools, but many other types of building are also used.

The ballot is secret, and the only people allowed in the polling station are the presiding officer (who is in charge), the polling clerks, the police on duty, the candidates, and their election agents and polling agents. All of these, except for the police officer on duty, must be given a written copy of the provisions of the Representation of the People Acts relating to the secrecy of the ballot. The presiding officer decides how many registered voters to admit at any one time.

The hours of voting are 07.00 to 22.00. Just before the poll opens, the presiding officer shows the ballot boxes to those at the polling station to prove that they are empty. The boxes are then locked and sealed.

In the polling station voters are directed to the presiding officer or poll clerk, who asks the voter his or her name, checks that it is on the register, and places a mark against the register entry. This records that the voter has received a ballot paper but does not show which one. The ballot papers are printed in books with counterfoils; serial numbers are printed on the back of each paper and each counterfoil. The officer or clerk also writes the voter's number on the counterfoil of the ballot paper and gives it an official mark before handing the paper to the voter. The official mark is intended to show that the papers placed in the ballot box are genuine. The paper lists the names of the candidates in alphabetical order, with a brief description of the candidate or his or her political party.

Voting takes place in a booth, which is screened to maintain secrecy. The voter marks the ballot paper with a cross in the box opposite the name of the candidate of his or her choice, and folds the paper to conceal the vote before placing it in the ballot box.

A paper which is spoiled by mistake must be returned to the presiding officer. If the presiding officer is satisfied that the spoiling was accidental, another paper is provided and the first cancelled. At the end of the voting the presiding officer delivers those spoilt papers to the returning officer. People who are unable to read, or are physically incapacitated, may have their ballot paper marked for them by a presiding officer. A blind person may also be assisted by a companion.

The poll must not be closed before the statutory time for any temporary purpose—for example, a lunch break—and once closed it cannot be reopened. After the poll closes, votes can only be accepted from voters who have already received ballot papers. Before the ballot boxes are removed from the polling station they are sealed to prevent further ballot papers being added. In the presence of the candidates' agents, the presiding officers make up the following into packages on which they are able to place their seal (the polling agents may also affix seals on behalf of the candidates):

—the ballot box unopened with its key attached;

—unused and spoilt ballot papers;

—the 'tendered' votes list, comprising 'tendered' ballot papers[1] and other votes which have been recorded by the presiding officer because of voters' physical incapacity;

—the marked copy of the register of voters;

—the counterfoils of the used ballot papers; and

—certificates showing that polling staff and police were on duty at the polling stations.

These packages are then delivered by the presiding officer or another approved person to the returning officer, together with a statement (known as the ballot paper account) accounting for the number of ballot papers which the presiding officer has been given. These are shown as ballot papers 'issued and not otherwise accounted for', 'unused' or 'spoilt or tendered'.

Postal Voting

Postal ballot papers, together with a declaration of identity, ballot paper envelopes and return postal envelopes are sent to people entitled to vote by post. Votes must reach the returning officer by the close of the poll. In addition to the returning officer and staff, candidates and their agents may be present when postal votes are issued and received. Special postal ballot

---

[1] 'Tendered' ballot papers are issued to people claiming to be particular electors named in the register after another person making the same claim has already voted. Instead of being put into the ballot box, the paper must be given to the presiding officer, endorsed with the voter's name and number in the register, and set aside in a separate packet. The voter's name and number in the register must be entered on a 'tendered voters list'. Tendered votes remain sealed unless the result of an election is brought into question.

boxes are provided for the returned postal envelopes, which should contain the declaration of identity and the sealed ballot paper envelope enclosing the ballot paper. The boxes are locked and sealed by the returning officer and agents who wish to affix their seal.

The ballot boxes are opened in the presence of the agents. The outer envelopes are opened, and the declarations of identity checked against the ballot paper envelopes. Special procedures are followed to prevent abuse of the system. The ballot paper envelopes are then opened and the postal ballot papers are placed in a locked and sealed ballot box, which is treated as an ordinary ballot box in the count. The papers are mixed with ordinary ballot papers and, apart from a different perforation mark, are identical to them.

The Count

The votes must be counted as soon as practicable after the poll at a place chosen by the returning officer. In addition to the returning officer and staff, the following people have the right to be present at the count: the candidates and their husbands or wives; and the candidates' election agents and counting agents. Counting agents may be appointed by candidates before the beginning of the poll. They watch the counting of the votes and check for errors; their number must be the same for each candidate and may be limited by returning officers. Other visitors, including journalists, may attend only if returning officers are satisfied that the official counting of the votes will not be impeded. If possible they will consult the election agents.

The returning officer may begin counting the ballot papers before all the ballot papers have been received. The seals are examined before the boxes are opened and emptied, and the total number of papers in each box is counted. The ballot paper account (see p. 38) is then checked in the presence of the election agents and the papers are then mixed together and sorted according to the candidates for whom they are marked. Counting assistants usually work in pairs in the presence of the candidates' agents. Doubtful papers are put aside, and the returning officer decides whether they are valid. If the result is close, candidates or their election agents may seek a recount; the decision is made by the returning officer. If the number of votes is equal, the winner is decided by drawing lots.

Declaration of the Result

The returning officer declares the result of the poll, usually in public. Most results are known within five or six hours of the close of poll. The remainder, mainly in rural constituencies, are declared in the next day or so. If the candidate elected is alleged to be disqualified or to have committed malpractices, the returning officer still declares the candidate to be elected. Objectors may then seek their remedy by election petition (see below).

After the election, the returning officer must notify the Clerk of the Crown[2] of the name of the candidate elected. This is done by adding to the original writ a certificate stating which candidate has been elected.

---

[2] In Northern Ireland, the Clerk of the Crown for Northern Ireland.

Election Petitions

People wishing to question the conduct or result of an election must do so by presenting an election petition. In England, Wales and Northern Ireland election petitions are presented to the High Court in the Queen's Bench Division. In Scotland they are presented to the Court of Session.

The petitioner must have been either an elector or a candidate in the election. The petition must set out the grounds of the complaint and is tried by two judges sitting in open court without a jury. In normal circumstances the hearing must take place within the constituency concerned. If a successful candidate is found to be guilty, through either his or her own actions or through his or her agent's actions, the election is void. The election is also void if the candidate was not qualified or if serious irregularities may have affected the result.

Appendix 1
General Election Results 1945–87

The following tables show the results of the 13 general elections held between 1945 and 1987. Redistribution of seats took place in 1950, 1955, 1974 and 1983.

Table 1: General Election Result 1945 (5 July)

Party	Votes cast	MPs elected	Candidates	% Share of total vote
Labour	11,995,152	393	604	47·8
Conservative	9,988,306	213	624	39·8
Liberal	2,248,226	12	306	9·0
Communist	102,780	2	21	0·4
Common Wealth	110,634	1	23	0·4
Others	640,880	19	104	2·0
Total	25,085,978	640	1,682	100·0

Electorate 33,240,391 Turnout 72·7%

Table 2: General Election Result 1950 (23 February)

Party	Votes cast	MPs elected	Candi- dates	% Share of total vote
Labour	13,266,592	315	617	46·1
Conservative	12,502,567	298	620	43·5
Liberal	2,621,548	9	475	9·1
Communist	91,746	0	100	0·3
Others	290,218	3	56	1·0
Total	28,772,671	625	1,868	100·0

Electorate 33,269,770 Turnout 84·0%

Table 3: General Election Result 1951 (25 October)

Party	Votes cast	MPs elected	Candi- dates	% Share of total vote
Conservative	13,717,538	321	617	48·0
Labour	13,948,605	295	617	48·8
Liberal	730,556	6	109	2·5
Communist	21,640	0	10	0·1
Others	177,329	3	23	0·6
Total	28,595,668	625	1,376	100·0

Electorate 34,645,573 Turnout 82·5%

Table 4: General Election Result 1955 (26 May)

Party	Votes cast	MPs elected	Candi- dates	% Share of total vote
Conservative	13,286,569	344	623	49·7
Labour	12,404,970	277	670	46·4
Liberal	722,405	6	110	2·7
Communist	33,144	0	17	0·1
Others	313,410	3	39	1·1
Total	26,760,498	630	1,409	100·0

Electorate 34,858,263 Turnout 76·7%

Table 5: General Election Result 1959 (8 October)

Party	Votes cast	MPs elected	Candi- dates	% Share of total vote
Conservative	13,749,830	365	625	49·4
Labour	12,215,538	258	621	43·8
Liberal	1,638,571	6	216	5·9
Plaid Cymru	77,571	0	20	0·3
Communist	30,897	0	18	0·1
Scottish National	21,738	0	5	0·1
Others	12,464	1	31	0·4
Total	27,859,241	630	1,536	100·0

Electorate 35,397,080 Turnout 78·8%

Table 6: General Election Result 1964 (15 October)

Party	Votes cast	MPs elected	Candi- dates	% Share of total vote
Labour	12,205,814	317	628	44·1
Conservative	12,001,396	304	630	43·4
Liberal	3,092,878	9	365	11·2
Plaid Cymru	69,507	0	23	0·3
Scottish National	64,044	0	15	0·2
Communist	45,932	0	36	0·2
Others	168,422	0	60	0·6
Total	27,655,374	630	1,757	100·0

Electorate 35,892,572 Turnout 77·1%

Table 7: General Election Result 1966 (31 March)

Party	Votes cast	MPs elected	Candi- dates	% Share of total vote
Labour	13,064,951	363	621	47·9
Conservative	11,418,433	253	629	41·9
Liberal	2,327,533	12	311	8·5
Scottish National	128,474	0	20	0·2
Communist	62,112	0	57	0·2
Plaid Cymru	61,071	0	20	0·2
Others	170,569	2	331	0·6
Total	27,263,606	630	1,707	100·0

Electorate 35,964,684 Turnout 75·8%

Table 8: General Election Result 1970 (18 June)

Party	Votes cast	MPs elected	Candi- dates	% Share of total vote
Conservative	13,145,123	330	628	46·4
Labour	12,179,341	287	624	43·0
Liberal	2,117,035	6	332	7·5
Scottish National	306,802	1	65	1·1
Plaid Cymru	175,016	0	36	0·6
Communist	37,970	0	58	0·1
Others	383,511	6	94	1·4
Total	28,344,798	630	1,837	100·0

Electorate 39,342,013 Turnout 72·0%

Table 9: General Election Result 1974 (28 February)

Party	Votes cast	MPs elected	Candi- dates	% Share of total vote
Labour	11,639,243	301	623	37·1
Conservative	11,868,906	297	623	37·9
Liberal	6,063,470	14	517	19·3
Scottish National	632,032	7	70	2·0
Plaid Cymru	171,364	2	36	0·6
National Front	76,865	0	54	0·3
Communist	32,741	0	44	0·1
Northern Ireland parties	717,986	12	48	2·3
Others	131,059	2	120	0·4
Total	31,333,226	635	2,135	100·0

Electorate 39,798,899 Turnout 78·7%

Table 10: General Election Result 1974 (10 October)

Party	Votes cast	MPs elected	Candidates	% Share of total vote
Labour	11,457,079	319	623	39·2
Conservative	10,464,817	277	623	35·8
Liberal	5,346,754	13	619	18·3
Scottish National	839,617	11	71	2·9
Plaid Cymru	166,321	3	36	0·6
National Front	113,843	0	90	0·4
Communist	17,426	0	29	0·1
Northern Ireland parties	702,094	12	43	2·4
Others	81,227	0	118	0·3
Total	29,189,178	635	2,252	100·0

Electorate 40,072,971 Turnout 72·8%

Table 11: General Election Result 1979 (3 May)

Party	Votes cast	MPs elected	Candi- dates	% Share of total vote
Conservative	13,697,690	339	622	43·9
Labour	11,532,148	269	523	36·9
Liberal	4,313,811	11	577	13·8
Scottish National	504,259	2	71	1·6
Plaid Cymru	132,544	2	36	0·4
National Front	190,747	0	303	0·6
Ecology	38,116	0	53	0·1
Communist	15,938	0	38	0·1
Workers Revolutionary	13,535	0	60	0·1
Northern Ireland parties	695,889	12	64	2·2
Others	85,338	0	129	0·3
Total	31,220,010	635	2,576	100·0

Electorate 41,093,264 Turnout 76·0%

Table 12: General Election Result 1983 (9 June)

Party	Votes cast	MPs elected	Candi- dates	% Share of total vote
Conservative	13,012,602	397	633	42·4
Labour	8,457,124	209	633	27·6
Liberal-Social Democratic Alliance[a]	7,780,577	23	633	25·4
Scottish National	331,975	2	72	1·1
Plaid Cymru	125,309	2	38	0·4
Ecology	54,102	0	109	0·2
National Front	27,053	0	60	0·1
British National	14,321	0	53	0·0
Communist	11,596	0	35	0·0
Workers Revolutionary	3,800	0	21	0·0
Northern Ireland parties[b]	763,474	17	94	2·5
Others	87,962	0	198	0·3
Total	30,669,895	650	2,579	100·0

Electorate 42,197,344 Turnout 72·7%

[a] Seventeen Liberal members were elected out of 322 candidates and six SDP members out of 311 candidates.

[b] All figures exclude the Ecology Party candidate in Antrim N., who is included in the Ecology figures.

Table 13: General Election Result 1987 (11 June)

Party	Votes cast	MPs elected	Candi- dates	% Share of total vote
Conservative[a]	13,763,066	376	633	42·3
Labour	10,029,944	229	633	30·8
Liberal-Social Democratic Alliance[b]	7,341,152	22	633	22·6
Scottish National	416,873	3	71	1·3
Plaid Cymru	123,589	3	38	0·4
Green	89,753	0	134	0·3
Communist	6,078	0	19	0·0
Northern Ireland parties	730,152	17	77	2·5
Others	32,463	0	87	0·1
Total	32,536,137	650	2,325	100·0

Electorate 43,181,321 Turnout 75·3%

[a] These figures include the Speaker of the House of Commons, who stood as 'Mr Speaker seeking re-election'. He was, before his election as Speaker, a Conservative member.

[b] Seventeen Liberal members were elected out of 327 candidates and five SDP members out of 306 candidates.

Sources: All figures in the above tables are taken from Butler and Kavanagh: *The British General Election of 1987* and Butler D and G: *British Political Facts 1900–1985* (see Further Reading).

Table 14: Northern Ireland Parties Result 1987 (11 June)

Party	Votes cast	MPs elected	Candi- dates	% Share of total vote
Ulster Unionist	276,230	9	12	37·8
Social Democratic & Labour	154,087	3	13	21·1
Democratic Unionist	85,642	3	4	11·7
Sinn Fein	83,389	1	14	11·4
Ulster Popular Unionist	18,420	1	1	2·5
Others	112,384	0	33	15·4
Total	730,152	17	77	100·0

Electorate 1,089,160   Turnout 67·0%

Table 15: Percentage Distribution of Votes Cast in each Region by Main Parties in the 1987 General Election

	Conservative	Labour	Alliance
England	**46·2**	**29·5**	**23·8**
North	32·3	46·4	21·0
Yorkshire and Humberside	37·4	40·6	21·7
East Midlands	48·6	30·0	21·0
East Anglia	52·1	21·7	25·7
South East	52·2	22·3	25·0
South West	50·6	15·9	33·0
West Midlands	45·5	33·3	20·8
North West	38·0	41·2	20·6
Wales	**29·5**	**45·1**	**19·9**
Scotland	**24·0**	**42·4**	**19·2**

Sources: *The British General Election of 1987*, by D. Butler and D. Kavanagh and *Times Guide to the House of Commons June 1987* (see Further Reading).

State of the Parties in the House of Commons in September 1991

As a result of by-elections since the 1987 general election, and following the merger between the Liberal and Social Democratic parties, the distribution of seats in the House of Commons in mid-September 1991 was: Conservative 368, Labour 227, Liberal Democrats 21, Social Democrats 3, Scottish National 5,[1] Plaid Cymru 3, Ulster Unionist 9, Democratic Unionist 3, Ulster Popular Unionist 1, Social Democratic and Labour 3, Sinn Fein 1, vacant 2. Not included are the Speaker and his three deputies (the Chairman of Ways and Means and the first and second Deputy Chairman of Ways and Means) who do not vote except in their official capacity in the event of a tie. The Sinn Fein member has not taken his seat.

[1] One former Labour member joined the Scottish National Party in 1990.

Appendix 2
By-Elections and New MPs
Elected since the General Election
of June 1987

Details of the 21 parliamentary by-elections held since the 1987 general election are given below.

Of the 21 vacancies, 12 arose in seats previously held by Labour MPs, 8 in former Conservative seats and one in a Northern Ireland seat formerly held by an Ulster Unionist MP. In the resulting by-elections the Conservatives retained 3 seats and lost 5, 3 to the Labour Party and 2 to the Liberal Democrats. In addition, the Labour Party retained 11 seats and lost one seat to the Scottish National Party. The Ulster Unionists retained their seat in Upper Bann.

Constituency	Cause of by-election and size of former MP's majority (MP's party in brackets)	Date of by-election	New MP and size of new MP's majority (MP's party in brackets)
Kensington	Death of Sir Brandon Rhys Williams (Conservative) 4,447	14.7.88	Mr Dudley Fishburn (Conservative) 815
Glasgow Govan	Resignation of Rt Hon Bruce Millan (Labour) 19,509	10.11.88	Mr James Sillars (Scottish National) 3,554
Epping Forest	Death of Sir John Biggs-Davison (Conservative) 21,513	15.12.88	Mr Steven Norris (Conservative) 4,504
Pontypridd	Death of Mr Brynmor John (Labour) 17,277	23.2.89	Dr Kim Howells (Labour) 10,794

Constituency	Cause of by-election and size of former MP's majority (MP's party in brackets)	Date of by-election	New MP and size of new MP's majority (MP's party in brackets)
Richmond (Yorkshire)	Resignation of Rt Hon Leon Brittan (Conservative) 19,576	23.2.89	Mr William Hague (Conservative) 2,634
Vale of Glamorgan	Death of Sir Raymond Gower (Conservative) 6,251	4.5.89	Mr John Smith (Labour) 6,028
Glasgow Central	Death of Mr Robert McTaggart (Labour) 17,253	15.6.89	Mr Michael Watson (Labour) 6,402
Vauxhall	Resignation of Mr Stuart Holland (Labour) 9,019	15.6.89	Ms Kate Hoey (Labour) 9,766

Constituency	Cause of by-election and size of former MP's majority (MP's party in brackets)	Date of by-election	New MP and size of new MP's majority (MP's party in brackets)
Mid Staffordshire	Death of Mr John Heddle (Conservative) 14,654	22.3.90	Mrs Sylvia Heal (Labour) 9,449
Upper Bann	Death of Mr Harold McCusker (Ulster Unionist) 17,361	17.5.90	Mr David Trimble (Ulster Unionist) 13,849
Bootle	Death of Mr Allan Roberts (Labour) 24,477	24.5.90	Mr Michael Carr (Labour) 23,517
Knowsley South	Death of Mr Sean Hughes (Labour) 20,846	27.9.90	Mr Edward O'Hara (Labour) 11,367
Eastbourne	Death of Mr Ian Gow (Conservative) 16,923	18.10.90	Mr David Bellotti (Liberal Democrat) 4,550

Constituency	Cause of by-election and size of former MP's majority (MP's party in brackets)	Date of by-election	New MP and size of new MP's majority (MP's party in brackets)
Bootle	Death of Mr Michael Carr (Labour) 23,517	8.11.90	Mr Joseph Benton (Labour) 19,465
Bradford North	Death of Mr Patrick Wall (Labour) 1,633	8.11.90	Mr Terrence Rooney (Labour) 9,514
Paisley North	Death of Mr Allen Adams (Labour) 14,442	29.11.90	Mrs Irene Adams (Labour) 3,770
Paisley South	Death of Mr Norman Buchan (Labour) 15,785	29.11.90	Mr Gordon McMaster (Labour) 5,030

Constituency	Cause of by-election and size of former MP's majority (MP's party in brackets)	Date of by-election	New MP and size of new MP's majority (MP's party in brackets)
Ribble Valley	Elevation to the peerage of Rt Hon David Waddington (Conservative) 19,528	7.3.91	Mr Mike Carr (Liberal Democrat) 4,601
Neath	Death of Mr Donald Coleman (Labour) 20,578	4.4.91	Mr Peter Hain (Labour) 9,830
Monmouth	Death of Sir John Stradling Thomas (Conservative) 9,350	16.5.91	Mr Huw Edwards (Labour) 2,406
Liverpool Walton	Death of Mr Eric Heffer (Labour) 23,253	4.7.91	Mr Peter Kilfoyle (Labour) 6,860

Appendix 3
Elections to the European
Parliament

The European Parliament, one of the four principal institutions of the European Community,[1] has 518 directly elected members (Members of the European Parliament—MEPs). Britain, together with each of the three other large member states (France, Germany and Italy), has 81 seats. The Parliament was originally a nominated body. The first elections took place in June 1979, and elections are held in each member state every five years, the most recent being in June 1989.

Of the 81 representatives from Britain, 66 are elected in England, eight in Scotland, four in Wales and three in Northern Ireland.[2] In England, Scotland and Wales voting is by the simple majority system in large single-member constituencies. In Northern Ireland the three representatives are elected in one constituency by the single transferable vote system of proportional representation.

---

[1] The other three are the Council of Ministers, the European Commission and the Court of Justice. For further details see FCO reference pamphlet *Britain in the European Community*, No 73/90, and FCO reference paper *Elections to the European Parliament*, No 235/89.

[2] In the election of June 1989 the Labour Party won 45 seats, the Conservative Party 32 and the Scottish National Party one seat. The other three seats were won in Northern Ireland by the Democratic Unionist, the Social Democratic and Labour, and the Ulster Unionist parties.

Electoral Arrangements

In Britain the method of electing representatives to the European Parliament is similar to that for parliamentary elections. The same polling stations are used and the same procedures are followed.

The boundaries of the European constituencies are drawn up by the Boundary Commissions in England, Scotland and Wales (see p. 5); each constituency is made up of between seven and nine parliamentary constituencies. Northern Ireland is a separate, single three-member constituency. The 66 European constituencies in England have an average electorate of about 550,000, the eight Scottish constituencies an average of about 500,000 and the four Welsh constituencies an average of about 540,000. The size of the electorate in Northern Ireland is about 1 million.

The same people are able to vote in the European elections as in parliamentary elections; in addition, peers who are members of the House of Lords have the vote. Voting in the European elections in Britain, as in all types of elections, is voluntary.

The qualifications for standing for election to the European Parliament are similar to those for parliamentary elections, although peers and clergy of the Churches of England, Scotland and Ireland and of the Roman Catholic Church may stand.

Candidates must be nominated by 30 individual electors, and are required to make a deposit of £1,000. This is returned if they receive 5 per cent of the valid votes cast in the constituency or, in Northern Ireland, one-quarter of the electoral quota at any stage in the count during the single transferable vote election.

The regulations for conduct of the elections to the European Parliament provide more time for the formal stages of the campaign than at parliamentary elections. With the exception of petty and personal expenses, the election expenses for each candidate can be up to £10,000 plus 4·3p for each elector on the electoral register. In addition, during the election campaign the candidate can claim the same entitlements, covering such items as free postage and the use of meeting halls, as in parliamentary elections (see pp. 22 and 27).

Further Reading

£

BOGDANOR, VERNON.
Multi-Party Politics and the Constitution.
ISBN 0 521 27526 1.
Paperback.　　　　Cambridge University Press　1983　3·00

BUTLER, DAVID and KAVANAGH, DENNIS.
The British General Election of 1987.
ISBN 0 333 46793 0. Paperback.　　　　Macmillan　1988　17·50

BUTLER, DAVID and GARETH.
British Political Facts 1900–1985.
ISBN 0 333 39949 8. Paperback.　　　　Macmillan　1986　20·99

BUTLER, DAVID and STOKES, DONALD.
Political Change in Britain: Basis of Electoral Choice.
ISBN 0 333 22600 3. Paperback.　　　　Macmillan　1975　10·99

CREWE, IVOR and HARROP, MARTIN (ed.).
Political Communications: The General Election Campaign of 1987.　　　Cambridge
ISBN 0 521 36403 5.　　　　University Press　1989　30·00

JOHNSTON, R.J.
Developments in Electoral Geography.
ISBN 0 415 04133 3.　　　　Routledge　1990　35·00

NORRIS, PIPPA.
British By-Elections. The Volatile Electorate.
ISBN 0 19 827330 4.　　　　Clarendon　1990　35·00

PARKER, F.R.
Parker's Conduct of Parliamentary Elections.
ISBN 0 853 14350 1.   Charles Knight   1983   89·00

The Times Guide to the European Parliament 1989.
ISBN 0 7230 0336 X.   Times Books   1989   25·00

The Times Guide to the House of Commons 1987.
ISBN 0 7230 0298 3.   Times Books   1987   20·00

Parliament.
ISBN 0 11 701631 4.   HMSO   1991

Elections to the European Parliament.
FCO, reference paper, No 235/89   1989

Organisation of Political Parties.
ISBN 0 11 7016489.   HMSO   1991

Representation of the People Act 1983.
ISBN 0 10 540283 4.   HMSO   1983   9·15

Representation of the People Act 1985.
ISBN 0 10 545085 5.   HMSO   1985   4·70

Representation of the People Act 1989.
ISBN 0 10 542889 2.   HMSO   1989   1·50

Forthcoming Publications
Forthcoming titles in the Aspects of Britain series will cover Britain's system of government, the Civil Service and executive agencies.

Written by Reference Services,
Central Office of Information

Printed in the UK for HMSO.
Dd 295002 c50 11/91